A Soul Song

Rochelle Simon

BookLeaf
Publishing

India | USA | UK

Presentation by *BookLeaf Publishing*

Web: www.bookleafpub.com

E-mail: info@bookleafpub.com

ISBN:9789360943523

First edition 2024

DEDICATION

To my soul connections, you have made my life
a beautiful song.

ACKNOWLEDGEMENT

I am deeply grateful to all who have contributed to making me what I have become today. The ones who continue to believe in me and encourage me to push my limits and go beyond. I have been blessed with a fantastic family who are my dearest critics and a treasure trove of friends and well wishers without whom I would not have mustered the courage to forge ahead.

My special thanks to colleagues past and present who have been a lifeline of support and strength throughout my journey.

PREFACE

This book is a capsule of the emotional intelligence and energies of the poet. The inner movements of a free and independent spirit providing a perspective on life, love, relationships and the little things that matter.

It is an opportunity to explore creatively what has been at the core of the soul. Love is a powerful force that when fueled by passion allows you to conquer anything. Magical things happen when you allow yourself to dream and act positively to make the dream a reality.

Writing this book has been a dream come true for me. It came at the right time when a confluence of emotions besieged my being at once propelling me to action. Gratitude is another powerful emotion that brings to life divine dreams that we see in hindsight.

A Stirring in my Soul

You enter my life and there is light
My whole world all of a sudden bright
You smile and like a wave on a roll
I feel a stirring in my soul.

Leaving me breathless with your words
Your voice falls softly upon me like the chorus
of the birds
As refreshing as chilled ice cubes in a bowl
I can surely feel a stirring in my soul.

I thank you from the depths of my heart
You fill my days and have become of them a
vital part
Bit by bit you have healed my brokenness and
made me whole
You have ignited that fire that is stirring in my
soul.

Belonging

Why does my heart feel numb?
Every time you travel miles away
Why do I wait restlessly scanning the grey
Cloudy horizon willing you to come.

'Return speedily to me',
I cry out in my sleep
The loneliness cannot be expressed
Emotions run too deep.

Now the day has arrived
You are back by my side
I feel like a whole person again
Forgetting every tear I cried.

Your fingers fill the empty gaps between mine
As we lie cozily entwined
Like two grains of sand in an hourglass of time
I will always be your Summer and you my sweet
Strawberry Wine!

Colours of my LOVE

My LOVE for you is a Kaleidoscope
Of colours that reflect dreams and hope
Like the seasons of life that ebb and flow
My LOVE for you is a constant glow!

Like a RED red rose in full bloom
My LOVE for you will dispel your gloom;

As comfortable as a pair of jeans in BLUE
My love for you is forever true!

Like a forest of rustling leaves all GREEN
When I whisper sweet nothings my LOVE for
you is seen.

And sometimes like a warm summers YELLOW
day
You will feel my LOVE as to the music we
sway!

When this life's journey we travel comes to its
twilight end
The colours of my LOVE for you like a rainbow
will blend.
Red, blue, green and yellow shine;

You know my LOVE you will forever be MINE!

Destiny

In the tapestry of time, the hands of fate weaves
A story book of life, like a tree with many leaves
Destiny's whisper like a guiding light
Leading us through sunny days and darkest
nights.

Like the dance of the stars, our winding paths
are drawn,
Bound by destiny from dusk till dawn
A road yet unseen, we walk along
Guided by fate like a silent song.

Through valley's deep and mountain's high
The call of destiny we cannot deny.
In every moment it's presence felt
With every twist our fate is dealt.

Yet in our hearts a flame bursts bright
The will to fight and conquer the night
For destiny's path is not set in stone,
But is shaped by the choices we make on our
own.

So let us embrace with open hearts
This gift of life with all its parts

For in the tapestry of destiny's design
It is surely our choices that will our futures
define.

Evenings in Chennai

Its that time of the day when traffic is at its peak
Bumper to bumper the variety of vehicles shriek
The sun dips low, painting an orange sky
But the tempers of drivers at choked signals are
at an all time high!

This is the scene every working day
But on the weekends happy crowds rush to the
Bay
To Marina Beach, a haven for all,
Stretched wide and far, its sands enthrall.

Families gather, children play,
As the waves dance to end the day.
Hawkers selling their wares come along
While teenagers waltz through the shore singing
a song.

The scent of jasmine fills the air,
As flower vendors string their lays and garlands
with care.
The sound of Carnatic music floats,
From concert halls to simple boats.

In the streets, the aroma of spices blend,

With the laughter of friends, a joyous trend.
The city comes alive with dancing lights,
A dazzling display, a myriad of sights.

From Adyar to Mylapore, the city glows,
In the tranquil embrace, the evening bestows.
Evenings in Chennai, are a time to unwind,
To cherish moments, to ease the mind.

In this vibrant city, where traditions thrive,
Evenings in Chennai, are a treasure to revive.
A more welcoming place on earth is hard to find
Where the food is fresh and spicy and the people
are one of a kind.

Flappy – The Little Pink Elephant

Deep in the forest, beside the silver lake
When the birds were asleep and the owls were
awake
A small little elephant was born
News of his arrival spread like wildfire at the
break of dawn.

Mrs. Duck came to see him with her brood of
ducklings
All in a row
Mr. Sparrow hopped along with Mrs. Sparrow in
tow,
'What shall we call him'? his papa trumpeted
aloud
Papa elephant was in his element, standing tall
and proud.

'Look mommy'! cried baby rabbit wanting to
have his say,
'Why is this baby elephant pink and not grey'?

Instantly there was a sudden hush, as all eyes
watched the little baby pink elephant.

While he softly flapped his little baby pink ears
Swish, Swish, Swish,
Swish, Swish, Swish he flapped them from side
to side,
As his mommy Mrs.Grey looked upon him with
love-filled eyes so wide.

Then with a loud trumpet papa elephant proudly
said: "He will be called FLAPPY"
As he stroked his baby's head.

'Flappy, flappy, flappy,' – the big brown toad
croaked!
'Flappy, flappy, flappy,' – chortled the baby
turtle, as in the soft mud he soaked.
'Flappy, flappy, flappy,' – the blue birds in the
cherry tree sang.
'Flappy, flappy, flappy, makes me so happy',
said baby rabbit in his baby rabbit twang!

Gratitude

Gratitude is a mindfulness that comes from
depths of a soul
It is that ingredient that makes a person feel
whole
There is always something to be grateful for, if
we took the time to see
The many things we are blest with will emerge
so clearly.

For every dawn that breaks, for every sunset's
glow,
For every gentle breeze, for every falling snow.
Gratitude whispers in the silence of the night
In the laughter of children, in their joys we
delight.

It's in the warmth of a hug, in a friend's kind
smile,
In the words of comfort that makes life
worthwhile
Gratitude finds a rhythm and dances in the rain,
In the melody of life, when we share someone's
pain.

It's in the food we eat, in the roof above our
heads,
In the shy lover's kiss that leave many words
unsaid.
Gratitude is a gift, a treasure to behold,
A reminder of the blessings, both big and
manyfold.

So let us pause and give thanks, for all we have
today,
For gratitude is the path to a heart that's light and
gay.
It renews a drooping spirit and energizes the
mind
When your heart is filled with Gratitude you will
always remain kind.

Happiness

What is happiness? how does it feel?
Where can I find it? Is it for real?
Its that feeling when laughter is shared with
friends
That emotion that creeps into us when with our
family we make amends.

Happiness is found in a child's squeal of joy
When her mother comes home with her
favourite toy,
It is found in the warmth of a lover's embrace
In the face of an athlete who has won the race.

Its in the giving, in the belonging
In what we love and all that we do
Happiness is the contentment we find
When we embrace what is pure and true.

Intelligence - Artificial vs Natural

In the crevices of the mind amidst grey matter
Two types of intelligence we find: natural - the
former; artificial - the latter.

One born of silicon, circuits ablaze,
The other of nature's intricate ways.

Artificial Intelligence - AI they say
Is definitely one of the marvels of our day.

Born of human ingenuity, on technology's stage
Programmed by algorithms and codes on a page.

Natural intelligence is the evolution of our kind
A symphony of neurons processing in the mind.

AI precise in its logical might,
Natural nuanced in creative flight.

One seeks to replicate, the other to explore
The many realms of knowledge, the heights to
which it can soar.

Yet in this common quest they find

A yearning for an understanding mind.

Artificial or natural, intelligence does not define
The essence of being human is where we draw
the line.

In this time - our digital age
AI has become all the rage

But let us not get carried away
For what truly matters is how we treat others
what we actually do and say!

Just between your soul and mine

Just between your soul and mine
An eternal bond, a secret entwined
In whispers soft emotions align
A sacred truth in the dance of time.

Weaving dreams together with hopes combined
Our souls commune in the realm that love
ignites,
In silence through space there is no fear
Whether near or far feelings are crystal clear.

Our spirits intertwine
In this place that's divine
An intoxication far more powerful than wine
Is the connection just between your soul and
mine.

Kindness

Kindness resides in a gentle heart
It blooms in small acts of gentleness of which it
is a core part
Like a word of comfort and a tear wiped away
A positive smile could brighten up someone's
day.

It is found in the warmth of a hug in a tender
reassuring touch
An expression of kindness does not ask for
much
Just a thread of compassion an understanding
nod
Showing someone in despair that they can still
hope in God.

Like a ray of sunshine kindness knows no
bounds
Its a universal language bringing magical sounds
Kindness is a gift we all can share
Its a treasure when you show someone how
much you care.

Love Unconditional

What is unconditional love?
Do we really know what it means;
Is there no measure, no limit, no condition that
binds it
A pure, divine, endless, ever-forgiving
composite.

A feeling blooming in souls like a flower,
Beyond measure, defying space and time with
steadfast power
It sees not flaws, beyond the skin
Embracing the emotions deep within.

Like a melody that knows no end
It whispers to the heart 'Take courage, Love has
no end',
When you experience life's dark night
It encourages with a hope that's strong and
bright.

Like the hand that reaches out and makes you
strong
In moments when everything seems to go wrong
Unconditional Love rears its head

And brings comfort with inspiring words that are
said.

Its the silent tears in prayer that are shed
The strength that comes when in faith we are led
Its the omnipresent force in the sub conscious
mind
That wipes away anxiety and pushing for a
solution to find.

Love unconditional is in a mother's warm
embrace
The kindness and forgiveness in a spouse's face.
The helping hand of a faithful friend
A gift from above that has no end.

Motherhood

A soulful strain is faintly heard,
Like the cooing of a mother bird
As she cradles her baby in loving warm arms
And is delighted by the sweet child's
mischievous charms.

With tender care she nurtures the child
Disciplining with love the spirit that's wild.
Teaching the basics and watching us grow
Lifting our hearts when we feel down and low.

Through sleepless nights and endless days
A mother's love with us always stays
She sacrifices her all for the child she has
birthed
In her selflessness there is no dearth.

So here's to the gift of Motherhood
A tested and tried combination of all that's good
Because the creator wanted to pour out His love
and care
He created the Mother filled with His goodness
everywhere!

Never Quit

When I'm faced with strife and dark thoughts loom
And all seems lost in shadowed gloom
There's still a spark within my soul
That refuses to let despondency take hold.

A voice that whispers 'Never Quit'
Though trials take me through this blinding pit,
For in my heart a strength resides
A higher power within me hides.

Though howling winds my ears may pierce
My lips repeat prayers with faith so fierce,
And through tears that fall from weeping eyes
My soul looks hard to see where the silver lining lies.

Keep courage when the world grows grim
And the light within you starts to dim,
With faith and confidence a fire can be lit
If we just remember to "Never Quit"!

On Turning 50

I turned 50! A milestone grand
It made me reflect and try to understand
The journey I'm on, the roads I've tread
The dreams I've chased, the tears I've shed.

At 50 I stand at a halfway mark
Between youthful vigour and wisdom's spark,
A time of transition, of change and shift
A moment to ponder life as a gift.

Gone are the days of wild wild youth
The many long years have brought depths of
truth
The lessons learned, the joys and sorrows
Have only made me stronger for all my
tomorrows.

50 years of laughter and tears
Of triumphs, defeats, hopes and fears
Here's to the 50 more ahead
Trusting in the divine wherever I'm led!

Prayer Verses

From early morning light
Till the dark of night
You protect me from every storm
Lord your presence is my lucky charm.

In moments through the day
Whether skies are clear or grey
When my path ahead is not so clear
You give me courage to overcome my fear.

Thank you Master for your love
For hope and encouragement from above
Wherever the future takes me Lord
I have no anxiety because you are my faithful
God!

Queen of hearts

There's a kingdom of cards where the roses
bloom red
There reigns a Queen with a gold crown on her
head,
A Queen of hearts with a gaze so bold
In a land where stories and legends unfold.

Her throne is of velvet her scepter so cold
Within her courts tales of wonder are told,
She rules with a grace that sets her apart
For her smile can thaw the cruelest of hearts.

But beware all you people in this land so fair
This Queen's temper is known to flare
With a cry of "Off with their heads" so often is
heard
Her punishment methods are royally feared.

Yet beneath all of this fearsome facade
Lies the heart of a queen that's not entirely hard
Love and loyalty she certainly holds dear
And on most sunny days she greets all with good
cheer

So raise a toast to this majestic Queen of Hearts

In popularity she is top of the charts
For in her life we find a reflection
Of Power, Love and Royal Perfection!

Rest with me a while

Rest with me a while my love
Beneath the shady boughs
Beside the bank where the river flows
Where we hear the calling of the turtle doves.

Rest a while with me my love
As the time slows down and a peace surrounds
On the grass that's lush and green
As the world fades and the noise dies
Find rest in the arms of your queen.

Cast your cares unto the wind
Let them blow your worry away
Lay your head on my lap and rest my Love
At the end of a trying day.

Feel the gentle breeze and the whisper of leaves
As you rest your weary soul
Let my calm embrace bring a smile to your face
And the warmth of my love make you
completely whole!

Song of my soul

27

The song of my soul is a melancholy strain
An echo of my emotions, a soulful refrain,
A symphony of joy, or lament of pain
An octave of notes, a collection insane.

It sings of love, of kindness too
Sometimes of disappointments that make me
feel blue,
But always finds a high note any day to end
No matter the sadness it will always with
courage blend.

Christmas Time

The Lights are going up!
Thanksgiving is in our hearts
Choirs and Carolers practicing
Pantomime volunteers play their parts.

Excited shoppers fill the malls
Families everywhere Deck the halls,
It's beginning to look a lot like Christmas
As you see the decorations
Go up on the walls.

Santa has started to fill up his sleigh
Children start counting down to the day
When under the Christmas tree they will see
Gifts galore for you and me.

We all have a Story

We all have a story, a tale to be told,
Of the joys we've experienced and the hardships
we've known.

Sometimes we wear our hearts on our sleeves
for all to see,
But often what's in them stays hidden as deep as
they can be.

So let us stay kind, for we never truly know,
The struggles and the battles that others undergo.

May empathy and compassion be the guiding
lights we share,
And may we always remember that each
storyteller deserves care.

For through this earthly journey, we all need
love and grace,
So let us stay kind to one another and create a
better place!